SNAKES

SNAKES

CHARTWELL
BOOKS, INC.

Published by Chartwell Books
A Division of Book Sales Inc.
114 Northfield Avenue
Edison, New Jersey 08837
USA

ISBN 0-7858-0981-3

This book is produced by
Quantum Books Ltd
6 Blundell Street
London N7 9BH

Project Manager: Rebecca Kingsley
Project Editor: Judith Millidge
Design/Editorial: David Manson
Andy McColm, Maggie Manson

The material in this publication previously appeared in
*Book of Snakes, Snakes of the World, Exotic Pet Survival
Guide*

QUMSPSN
Set in Futura
Reproduced in Singapore by Eray Scan
Printed in Singapore by Star Standard Industries (Pte) Ltd

Contents

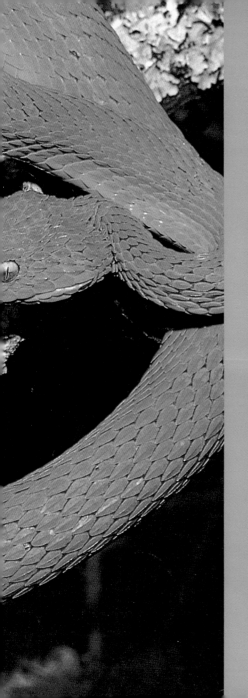

SUPERNATURAL SNAKES

Snakes have always held a great fascination for people, which has often bordered on an obsession. Since prehistoric times, snakes have been shrouded in mysticism and superstition. This fascination is due at least partly to their very strange shape and motion and their ability to strike unexpectedly with deadly accuracy. With such inhuman and 'unnatural' attributes people considered them to be supernatural and superhuman.

Snakes through History

Myths and legends about snakes abound, and they have been worshipped and used in ceremonies and rituals all over the world. The aborigines in Australia, who still practice rock painting, frequently depict snakes.

ANCIENT SNAKES

In the Bible, Adam and Eve are tricked by the serpent in the Garden of Eden into eating fruit from the tree of knowledge and consequently the Judeo-Christian view of the serpent is one of evil. By contrast, in ancient Egypt, snakes were revered as gods.

Egypt's economy depended on the Nile, and the Spirit of the Nile was a snake god. The snake symbolized the mighty power of the ruling Pharaoh. The most famous snake in Egypt was the asp, supposedly used in the suicide of Cleopatra, possibly an Egyptian Cobra or poisonous viper.

Left. The harmless Milk Snake mimics the warning coloration of the dangerous, highly poisonous coral snakes.

Above. The colors of the Texas Coral Snake provide a clear warning that the snake is dangerously venomous.

SNAKES IN MEDICINE

Eating the flesh of snakes is often thought to cure or at least prevent disease. The Chinese eat snakes as a cure for tuberculosis and in the US, rattlesnake oil was sold as a remedy. Snake venom has been used as a cure for gangrene, meningitis, cholera and as a blood coagulant. In 293 BC, a Roman plague was cured by the god of medicine, Aesculapius, who appeared in the form of a snake. Even today, the emblem of the medical profession is a staff with two entwined snakes.

SNAKEBITES

It is estimated that about 30,000 people worldwide die each year from snakebites mostly in poorer countries without medical care. In India, 10,000 people a year die from bites, in the US the number is less than 30. In Britain, you are more likely to die from a bee sting (6 a year) than a snakebite (1 since 1945). Snakebites can be prevented with a few simple precautions, such as not picking up unidentified snakes, being careful where you walk and also wearing adequate footwear.

S U P E R N A T U R A L   S N A K E S

Biology and Evolution

Long before humans and other mammals evolved, reptiles were spreading over all but the coldest parts of the world. Snakes are a highly successful group of reptiles that have colonized almost all habitats, since they first appeared at least 130 million years ago.

SNAKE BIOLOGY

Snakes have a number of features in common, making their biology rather consistent. They have all lost their limbs and their long cylinder-shaped bodies impose restrictions. All snakes are, to a greater or lesser extent, dependent on the warmth of the sun to maintain their temperature and to incubate their eggs or develop their young. Although some species are highly territorial, some have elaborate courtships and others hibernate communally, snakes generally lack the social behavior found in many birds, mammals and other groups of animals.

Left. The Fox Snake from the Great Lakes region in the US is a powerful constrictor, killing its prey by suffocation.

Above. The Paradise Flying Tree Snake has attractive markings which also act as very effective camouflage.

SNAKE FOSSILS

The earliest fossil remains which are recognizably of a snake were found in 130 million-year-old rocks in the Sahara in North Africa. The largest snake fossil found was an extinct python in Egypt, which may have measured as much as 60ft in length.

Relatively few snake fossils have been found as most fossils are of marine creatures. Since snakes lived mostly on land few have been preserved as fossils.

SNAKE EVOLUTION

There is little doubt that snakes evolved from lizards with some transitional forms appearing in the Cretaceous period – the great age of the dinosaurs. It was not until after the end of the dinosaurs, 65 million years ago, that snakes started to diversify and even today their evolution is still progressing. In geological terms, the snakes are still a new group, but with some 2,700 varied species around the world.

Snake Senses

Snakes gather information about the world in a very different way from us. While we rely mainly on sight and hearing, these senses are very poorly developed in snakes. Instead they depend on other stimuli, in particular scents and in some cases, heat.

SNAKE HEARING

Snakes are said to be deaf, because they lack outer ears and Eustachian tubes, and are unable to receive airborne sound waves. However, their inner ear reacts acutely to any ground vibrations which are detected by the lower jaw, in contact with the ground, and transmitted via the bones.

SNAKE EYESIGHT

Snake eyes are usually inefficient. They are unable to change the shape of the lens of the eye to focus and, most have no movable eyelids giving them an unblinking stare. Those active in the day usually have rounded pupils while nocturnal snakes, such as pythons, have vertical slit pupils.

Left. The Fierce Snake, reputed to be the most poisonous snake in the world, is confined to desert regions of Australia.

Above. The White-Lipped Pit Viper's heat sensitive pits between eye and nostril can clearly be seen.

SNAKE SENSE OF SMELL

Smell is the most important sense to snakes. Prey, predators and members of the opposite sex are identified by the scent chemicals they emit. Scent particles from the air are picked up and 'tasted' by the snake's forked tongue. The information is then transferred to the brain via special scent-sensitive cells in the snake's palate.

HEAT-SEEKING SNAKES

All snakes are sensitive to changes in their surrounding temperature and to infra-red radiation. Some boas, pythons and all pit vipers have special heat receptors, or sensory pits, on each side of their head, between the eye and the nostril enabling them to detect and accurately strike at warm-blooded prey, even in total darkness.

13

Snake Locomotion

Although we say that snakes 'crawl', they can actually move in four ways: serpentine movement, concertina movement, rectilinear movement and sidewinding. The type of movement depends largely on the terrain.

SERPENTINE LOCOMOTION

In serpentine movement, the snake's body is bent into horizontal loops by the contraction of muscles on the inner side of each loop. As the contractions move along the snake, a series of waves passes from the head backwards. On land, serpentine motion is only possible where there are stones or vegetation on the ground for the waves to push against, propelling the snake forward.

CONCERTINA LOCOMOTION

Concertina movement is used when crawling over difficult terrain or in a confined space such as a small rodent's burrow. The snake wedges the back part of its body and extends the rest of the body forward as far as possible. It then wedges the head and concertinas the front of the body, drawing itself forward. The snake then wedges the back part again and repeats the process.

Left. The Red Diamondback Rattlesnake is an inhabitant of extreme southern California and is extremely venomous.

Above. The Speckled King Snake has an immunity to rattlesnake venom and they specialize in eating them.

RECTILINEAR LOCOMOTION

Rectilinear creeping is used by large heavy snakes, particularly boas and pythons, and allows them to move in a straight line. The snake uses the muscles joining the ventral scales to the ribs and contracts them in waves down the body. The ventral scales grip onto irregularities in the ground and the snake is propelled forward in a seemingly effortless gliding motion.

SIDEWINDING

Sidewinding relies least on a firm surface to push against and is used by snakes living in desert areas with shifting sand surfaces. In sidewinding, the snake shifts itself by moving sideways in a series of steps at an angle of about 45° to its body. The snake lifts its head off the ground and thrusts it to the side with the body following it in a series of parallel lines.

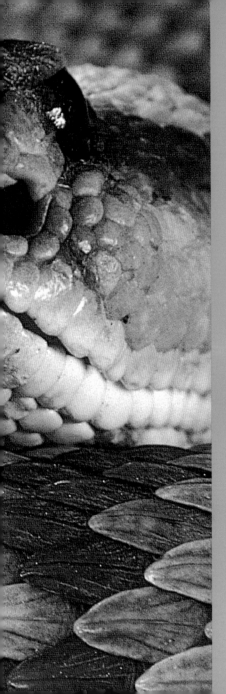

SNAKE SPECIES

Key to symbols
A number of icons are used to provide a snapshot of each snake. These are explained below.

Size (in)

Habitat

 Grassy areas scrub and heath   Semi-aquatic

 Woodlands   Aquatic

 Tropical forests   Mountains and caves

 Desert and arid areas   Buildings

Diet

 Rodents and small mammals   Birds

 Fish and amphibians   Eggs

Danger!
Venomous
Several species produce venom that is toxic and very dangerous to humans.
Treat all snakes with caution.

BOA/SUNBEAM SNAKE

SUNBEAM SNAKE

A shiny snake with smooth scales. The snout is shovel-shaped to allow the snake to burrow. The eyes are very small and round. The head is flattish. The underside is almost white, while the upperside is dark gray.

Scientific name *Xenopeltis unicolor.*
Size 39in.
Habitat Agricultural areas, parks forests, under debris.
Distribution SE Asia.
Food Lizards, other snakes, frogs, small rodents.
Breeding Egg-laying, 6 egg clutches.

COMMON BOA

A large boa species with variable markings. They are gray or beige with dark brown markings along the back. It has no heat pits.

Scientific name *Boa constrictor.*
Size 13ft.
Habitat Rain forest clearings, scrub, agricultural land, edges of villages.
Distribution S and C America, W Indian islands.
Food Mammals and birds.
Breeding Live-bearing, up to 50 young in a litter.

PACIFIC BOA

This snake may be light gray, almost white with an irregular dark line running along its back, or brick-red with a maroon line. They can either be thick-set or slim. The head is flattish and the snout is obliquely angled. It lacks heat pits.

Scientific name *Candoia carinata.*
Size 5ft.
Habitat Forests.
Distribution New Guinea.
Food Small mammals, birds, lizards.
Breeding Live-bearing, up to 70 young in a litter.

RUBBER BOA

A uniformly brown or olive colored cylindrical snake, with small shiny scales and small eyes. The tail is short and blunt and is often raised off the ground to deflect attacks from its head.

Scientific name *Charina bottae.*
Size 32in.
Habitat Scrub, grassland, pinewood, beneath bark and trees.
Distribution N America.
Food Snakes, birds, small rodents, small salamanders.
Breeding Live-bearing, 2–8 in a litter.

EMERALD TREE BOA

The young snakes are red or orange, but the color changes to green by the end of their first year of life. They have a row of white markings along their back and large prominent heat pits.

Scientific name *Corallus caninus*.
Size 5¹/4ft.
Habitat Tropical rain forests with large trees.
Distribution Amazon Basin in S America.
Food Small mammals and birds.
Breeding Live-bearing, up to 20 in a litter.

5¹/4ft

AMAZON TREE BOA

A slim snake whose color varies from brown, yellow, orange or gray. Some varieties have dark markings on their backs. The young snakes are more brightly colored than the adults. There are prominent heat pits.

Scientific name *Corallus enhydris*.
Size 6ft.
Habitat Forests with tall trees.
Distribution S America, W Indies, Central America.
Food Small mammals, frogs, birds, lizards.
Breeding Live-bearing, up to 20 young.

6ft

BRAZILIAN RAINBOW BOA

This is one of the most colorful of the nine subspecies of rainbow boa which exist. The scales are glossy and iridescent. There is a row of black circles down the back and black 'eyespots' along each side. It has shallow heat pits.

Scientific name *Epicrates cenchria cenchria*.
Size 6^1/$_2$ft.
Habitat Tropical forests and clearings.
Distribution S America.
Food Small mammals, birds.
Breeding Live-bearing, up to 30 young.

HAITIAN BOA

A variable snake with blotches along the back. The color of the blotches can be dark gray, brown or reddish. The ground color is lighter, pale gray. There are shallow heat pits.

Scientific name *Epicrates striatus*.
Size 7^1/$_2$ft.
Habitat Forests and mangroves. Likes to climb up into thatched roofs.
Distribution Haiti, Bahamas.
Food Young eat lizards, adults eat chickens, small mammals, birds.
Breeding Live-bearing, up to 50 young.

B O A S

ROUGH-SCALED SAND BOA

The most attractively marked member of
this genus, with a distinctive dark
zigzag pattern running along the back.
The scales are raised, hence its name.
This is snake which frequently burrows
during the day.

Scientific name *Eryx conicus*.
Size 39in.
Habitat Sandy, desert areas.
Distribution Sri Lanka, Pakistan,
India.
Food Rodents, birds, lizards.
Breeding Live-bearing, up to 11
young in a litter.

YELLOW ANACONDA

A snake with yellow coloring and an
attractive pattern of large black
blotches along the back and along the
flanks. The eyes point upwards. It has
no heat pits.

Scientific name *Eunectes notaeus*.
Size 6¹/2ft.
Habitat Swamps.
Distribution S America.
Food Reptiles, birds, mammals.
Breeding Live-bearing, with large
litters.

BAJA CALIFORNIAN ROSY BOA

A heavily bodied snake with a narrow head and blunt tail. It has stripes running down the length of the body which are orange or brownish-orange and well-defined. The eyes are also orange. There are no heat pits.

Scientific name *Lichanura trivirgata saslowi.*
Size 39in.
Habitat Lava flows, rocky areas.
Distribution Mexico.
Food Birds, small mammals.
Breeding Live-bearing, litters of 3–8 young.

39in

JAVELIN SAND BOA

A snake with a short blunt tail, pale yellow, buff or gray in color. The irregular markings along its back can be bars or spots. There is a dark line running from the eye to the corner of the jaw. There are no heat pits.

Scientific name *Eryx jaculus.*
Size 32in.
Habitat Dry, sandy places, under rocks.
Distribution SE Europe, Turkey, Middle East.
Food Rodents, small birds, lizards.
Breeding Live-bearing, litters up to 20.

32in

PYTHONS

GREEN TREE PYTHON

A green snake with a long prehensile tail and a broad head. There are rows of small white spots along the back. The young snakes are bright sulfur yellow or red, changing to green by the age of two. There are prominent heat pits.

Scientific name *Chondropython viridis.*
Size 5ft.
Habitat Rain forests.
Distribution New Guinea.
Food Birds, mammals, bats. Young eat lizards.
Breeding Egg-laying, up to 26 eggs.

CHILDREN'S PYTHON

This is one of the smaller pythons. The head is narrow and the body is slender. Light brown upperside, almost white underneath. The scales are large and cover the heat pits.

Scientific name *Liasis childreni.*
Size 39in.
Habitat Plains and hills, near outcrops and woodland.
Distribution N Australia.
Food Small mammals, bats, frogs, lizards.
Breeding Egg-laying, 8–16 eggs.

BLACK-HEADED PYTHON

A python with a glossy black head and neck. The rest of the body is yellowish, buff or pinkish-brown with dark cross-bars. There are no heat pits.

Scientific name *Aspidites melanocephalus.*
Size 8¹/₂ft.
Habitat Tropical and subtropical grasslands and hills.
Distribution Australia.
Food Snakes, birds on the ground, small mammals.
Breeding Egg-laying, 5–10 eggs.

DIAMOND PYTHON

A snake that is usually black with a white spot on nearly every scale. Some areas can be completely black or white. There are heat pits around the mouth.

Scientific name *Morelia spilota spilota.*
Size 6¹/₂ft.
Habitat Woodland, rocky areas.
Distribution New South Wales, Australia.
Food Mammals, birds.
Breeding Egg-laying, up to 50 eggs.

CARPET PYTHON

A variable snake, usually brown or gray with paler bands of color crossing the body. There can be pale irregular blotches and streaks on the body. There is an almost black variety with yellow bands.

Scientific name *Morelia spilota variegata.*
Size 13ft.
Habitat Forests, scrub, rocky areas.
Distribution Australia, New Guinea.
Food Mammals, birds.
Breeding Egg-laying, up to 50 eggs.

BURMESE PYTHON

A large yellowish python with large blotches of chestnut brown. There is an arrow-shaped dark mark on the top of its head and a dark streak through each eye. There are heat pits.

Scientific name *Python molurus bivittatus.*
Size 23ft.
Habitat Tropical forests, fields.
Distribution India, Sri Lanka, Burma, Thailand.
Food Mammals, birds.
Breeding Egg-laying, up to 70 eggs.

ROYAL PYTHON

A strongly built python with a very dark background color. There are oval blotches on the back which are tan, pale brown or yellowish-brown. Along each flank there are a series of light-colored blotches. There are heat pits.

Scientific name *Python regius*.
Size 5ft.
Habitat Grasslands and riverbanks.
Distribution W Africa.
Food Small mammals, birds.
Breeding Egg-laying, up to 10 eggs.

5ft

RETICULATED PYTHON

Possibly the largest snake in the world. They have intricate markings of black diamonds with yellow edges, on a gray background. There are also irregular white patches along the flanks. There are heat pits.

Scientific name *Python reticulatus*.
Size 33ft.
Habitat Tropical forests and clearings, villages and towns.
Distribution SE Asia.
Food Mammals, birds, domestic livestock.
Breeding Egg-laying, up to 100 eggs.

33ft

AFRICAN PYTHON

A strong python with a wide head covered in scales. The color can be brown or greenish-brown with a row of dark markings on the back and flanks. There are heat pits.

Scientific name *Python sebae*.
Size 16ft.
Habitat Grasslands, rocky areas near villages and farms.
Distribution S Sahara in Africa.
Food Mammals, birds, crocodiles, fish.
Breeding Egg-laying, up to 50 eggs.

16ft

LONG NOSE TREE SNAKE

A very thin snake with an elongated head and a pointed snout. The eyes have horizontal pupils which allow the snake to judge distances accurately. The green color, along with the shape, provide efficient camouflage.

Scientific name *Ahaetulla nasuta*.
Size 6¹/₂ft.
Habitat Tropical forests.
Distribution SE Asia.
Food Lizards, frogs, small mammals.
Breeding Live-bearing, small litters.

6¹/₂ft

TRANS-PECOS RATSNAKE

A ratsnake with a slim body, narrow head and large eyes. The color can vary from tan, to buff or cream to pale yellow. There are dark markings along the back. They are active only at night.

Scientific name *Bogertrophis subocularis*.
Size 5¹/4ft.
Habitat Deserts, rocky semi-arid places.
Distribution USA, Mexico.
Food Small mammals, snakes, lizards.
Breeding Egg-laying, up to 20 eggs.

5¹/4ft

GLOSSY SNAKE

A slender snake with an almost cylindrical body and smooth shiny scales. There are pale brown or gray markings. The ground color can be pale tan, cream or brown. They are docile snakes and do not bite.

Scientific name *Arizona elegans*.
Size 5ft.
Habitat Grassland, scrub, open woods, deserts.
Distribution USA, Mexico.
Food Small mammals, snakes, lizards.
Breeding Egg-laying, up to 20 eggs.

5ft

HARMLESS BACK-FANGED SNAKES

HARMLESS BACK-FANGED SNAKES

PARADISE FLYING TREE SNAKE

Each scale is black with a yellow-green center. There are also some dark red markings along the back. A slender snake also known as the 'flying snake' as it can parachute from high branches by spreading out its ribs.

Scientific name *Chrysopelea paradisii.*
Size 39in.
Habitat Forests, gardens, trees and shrubs.
Distribution SE Asia.
Food Lizards, frogs, small rodents.
Breeding Egg-laying.

39ft

DARK GREEN WHIPSNAKE

A slim snake with large eyes. They are usually green or yellow with irregular dark crossbars on the back and sides. The tail area has broken stripes. There are some areas where these snakes are all black.

Scientific name *Coluber viridflavus.*
Size 6¹/2ft.
Habitat Dry, rocky areas, woods and fields.
Distribution Central Europe, Italy.
Food Lizards, small mammals, nestling birds.
Breeding Egg-laying.

6¹/2ft

SMOOTH SNAKE

A cylindrical snake with smooth scales. The head and the eyes are small. The color is usually gray with small brown spots running down the back. Mostly active by day, it kills its prey by constriction.

Scientific name *Coronella austriaca*.
Size 30in.
Habitat Heaths, open woods, railway embankments.
Distribution Europe, W Asia.
Food Lizards, small rodents.
Breeding Live-bearing, up to 10 young.

AFRICAN EGG-EATING SNAKE

A slim snake with keeled scales and a cylindrical body. The head is small with two V-shaped marks. The snout is very rounded. It is gray in color with large dark blotches along the back. The inside of the mouth is black.

Scientific name *Dasypeltis scabra*.
Size 39in.
Habitat Most areas, except deserts.
Distribution Africa, S of the Sahara.
Food Bird's eggs, swallowed whole, crushed and the empty shell rejected.
Breeding Egg-laying, up to 25 eggs.

AMERICAN RACER

A slender, fast moving snake with smooth scales. The colors include black, blue, gray, greenish, olive and brown, making this a difficult snake to identify. They are active by day.

Scientific name *Coluber constrictor*.
Size 5ft.
Habitat Fields, lake edges.
Distribution N and Central America.
Food Reptiles, birds and small mammals.
Breeding Egg-laying, up to 20 eggs.

SCARLET SNAKE

A burrowing snake with a cylindrical body. The head is pointed and small with smooth scales. It is brightly colored with bands of red, white and black on the back. The underside is white or cream.

Scientific name *Cemophora Coccinea*.
Size 16in.
Habitat Loose, sandy soil. Old logs.
Distribution SE USA.
Food Snakes and their eggs, lizards, mice.
Breeding Egg-laying.

RINGNECK SNAKE

A small, slim snake whose body is light gray to black. Behind the head, there is a yellow or orange band. The belly is orange and the tail is red underneath which is held up when frightened.

Scientific name *Diadophis punctatus*.
Size 30in.
Habitat Damp areas. Under logs.
Distribution N America.
Food Worms, amphibians, insects, small reptiles, slugs.
Breeding Egg-laying.

INDIGO SNAKE

A large, black snake with polished scales. The body is almost triangular. The chin can be red or dull white. The young snakes have more red on their undersides and bluish marks on their sides.

Scientific name *Drymarchon corais couperi*.
Size 6^{1}/2ft.
Habitat Sandy areas.
Distribution SE USA (Florida).
Food Fish, amphibians, reptiles, birds, small mammals.
Breeding Egg-laying, up to 10 eggs.

BLACK RAT SNAKE

These are shiny, black snakes. There are nine subspecies recognized, all have variable coloring and markings. The young sometimes keep the patterning they are born with – grayish with darker markings down their bodies.

Scientific name *Elaphe obsoleta.*
Size 6ft.
Habitat Savannah, trees.
Distribution N America to Mexico.
Food Small mammals, birds, rodents.
Breeding Egg-laying, up to 14 eggs.

CORN SNAKE

A handsome ratsnake with large red saddles on a gray or yellowish ground. There is a black border on each saddle and smaller spots on the flanks and there is always a V-shaped mark on the top of the head. The underside is black and white.

Scientific name *Elaphe guttata guttata.*
Size 6ft.
Habitat Woody or rocky areas. Good climbers.
Distribution SE and E USA.
Food Rodents, birds.
Breeding Egg-laying, up to 20 eggs.

FOX SNAKE

A strongly built ratsnake with bold patterning of dark chestnut-brown blotches down the back. The background is either gray or yellowish. There are smaller blotches on the flanks. The head may be rust-colored.

Scientific name *Elaphe vulpina*.
Size 51in.
Habitat Prairies, woods, swamps, farmland.
Distribution Central USA, Canada.
Food Small mammals.
Breeding Egg-laying.

51in

WESTERN HOGNOSE SNAKE

This snake has a distinct snout which is upturned. The scales are heavily keeled, giving a rough appearance. The color is usually light brown or gray with blotches of brown, reddish-brown or olive along the back. When frightened, it can pretend to be dead.

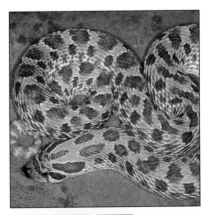

Scientific name *Herterodon nasicus*.
Size 28in.
Habitat Prairies, sandy soil.
Distribution USA, Canada, Mexico.
Food Rodents, amphibians.
Breeding Egg-laying, up to 15 eggs.

28in

HARMLESS BACK-FANGED SNAKES

EASTERN HOGNOSE SNAKE

Similar to the Western Hognose Snake but with several different color patterns. The color is usually brown or tan with blotches on the back and sides. Some species are pure black. The snake can play dead when threatened.

Scientific name *Heterodon paltyrhinos*.
Size 32in.
Habitat Sandy soil areas.
Distribution Central, E and SE USA.
Food Rodents, amphibians.
Breeding Egg-laying.

32in

SPOTTED NIGHT SNAKE

This is a small snake with smooth scales. The head is flattish and there are dark blotches along the back. The snake is light brown or gray in color. Behind the head, there is often a large dark patch, which can be divided into two areas. Active only at night.

Scientific name *Hypsiglena torquata*.
Size 24in.
Habitat Desert, scrub, meadows, woods.
Distribution S and SW USA.
Food Amphibians, small mammals.
Breeding Egg-laying, 2–9 eggs.

24in

PRAIRIE KING SNAKE

A cylindrical shaped snake with smooth scales. The head is small. The markings vary from gray with brown or reddish-brown oval blotches, to less regular blotches on the flanks. The markings can be indistinct of totally missing and the snake uniformly brown.

Scientific name *Lampropeltis calligaster.*
Size 39in.
Habitat Fields, prairies, forests.
Distribution Central and SE USA.
Food Small reptiles, rodents, birds.
Breeding Egg-laying, 6–15 eggs.

SPECKLED KING SNAKE

This snake is black with a yellow or white spot on each scale. These spots can form a pattern of bands. The shape of this snake is cylindrical with smooth shiny scales.

Scientific name *Lampropeltis getulus holbrooki.*
Size 6^1/2ft.
Habitat Moist and dry areas, swamps.
Distribution Central and S USA.
Food Lizards, snakes, birds, small mammals, amphibians.
Breeding Egg-laying, 6–20 eggs.

MEXICAN KING SNAKE

A snake with smooth scales and relatively thin. The background is gray with narrow saddles along the back, each a dark red color, edged in black. There is a red mark on top of the head.

Scientific name *Lampropeltis mexicana mexicana.*
Size 30in.
Habitat Mountains, in rocks and scrub.
Distribution NE Mexico.
Food Birds, small mammals.
Breeding Egg-laying, 4–10 eggs.

MILK SNAKE

This snake mimics the deadly coral snake with the red coloration, but is not a poisonous species. Their name is derived from a myth that they fed on cow's milk. They vary in appearance between areas, the most colorful are found in the southern most areas.

Scientific name *Lampropeltis triangulum.*
Size 51in.
Habitat Savannah.
Distribution E USA, S America.
Food Rodents, small mammals.
Breeding Egg-laying, 5–14 eggs.

BROWN HOUSE SNAKE

This snake has small, smooth scales and large eyes. It is uniformly colored reddish-brown, brown, orange or nearly black. There is a cream line running from the snout onto the neck. The underside is shiny and pinkish-white. They are powerful constrictors.

Scientific name *Lamprophis fulginosus.*
Size 39in.
Habitat Farmland, scrub, grassland.
Distribution Southern Africa.
Food Rodents, small mammals, lizards.
Breeding Egg-laying, 8–15 eggs.

MONTPELIER SNAKE

This snake has distinctive eyes and a muscular appearance. Their color varies through brown, rust, gray, olive to black. They are very aggressive and fast movers.

Scientific name *Malpolon monspessulanus.*
Size 6¹/₂ft.
Habitat Dry scrub, vineyards, marshes, open places.
Distribution Portugal, Spain, Balkans, N Africa. SW Asia, S France.
Food Snakes, lizards, small mammals.
Breeding Egg-laying.

SONORAN WHIP SNAKE

This snake has a streamlined head, and a slim body with large eyes. The body is gray or olive. A black line runs from the snout to just below each eye.

Scientific name *Masticophis bilineatus.*
Size 5¹/₄ft.
Habitat Mountain foothills in dry areas, among cacti, sparse trees.
Distribution SE Arizona.
Food Lizards, frogs, birds.
Breeding Egg-laying.

COACHWHIP SNAKE

This snake has smooth scales, large eyes and a long tail. The color can be brown, tan, gray or pinkish with bands on the front of the body. The scales on the tail give the impression of being plaited.

Scientific name *Masticophis flagellum.*
Size 8¹/₄ft.
Habitat Deserts, woods, farmland.
Distribution S USA, N Mexico.
Food Lizards, snakes, birds, small mammals
Breeding Egg-laying.

VIPERINE SNAKE

Young snakes are slender, adults are stockily built. The scales are keeled. The color can be olive, brown, greenish or reddish with two rows of dark blotches on the back. There may also be two pale yellow stripes down the back.

Scientific name *Natrix maura.*
Size 30in.
Habitat Close to water.
Distribution Spain, Portugal, N Africa.
Food Frogs, toads, tadpoles, earthworms.
Breeding Egg-laying.

GRASS SNAKE

This snake has keeled scales and is usually olive-brown. There are black bars or spots on each side. There can be pale, yellow stripes on the body. Behind the head, there are cream or yellow patches which can form a collar distinguishing this from similar snakes.

Scientific name *Natrix natrix.*
Size 5ft.
Habitat Damp meadows, banks of streams and canals, woods.
Distribution SW Asia, NW Africa, Europe.
Food Fish, amphibians.
Breeding Egg-laying, 20 eggs.

DICE SNAKE

A snake with heavily keeled scales and a narrow head. They are usually greenish, brown or gray, with spots over the back and sides. The nostrils and eyes point upwards.

Scientific name *Natrix tessellata*.
Size 39in.
Habitat Often seen in water.
Distribution Italy, SE Europe, Asia.
Food Fish, amphibians.
Breeding Egg-laying.

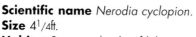

GREEN WATER SNAKE

This snake has strongly keeled scales. The head is triangular and the small eyes point upwards. The color is greenish-brown, with darker mottling.

Scientific name *Nerodia cyclopion*.
Size 4^1/4ft.
Habitat Swamps, banks of lakes, ponds.
Distribution Florida, Mississippi Basin.
Food Fish, amphibians.
Breeding Live-bearing, up to 50 young.

SMOOTH GREEN SNAKE

A slim green snake with smooth scales. The color is green on the surface and the undersides are white. The young can be olive or brown in color.

Scientific name *Opheodryas vernalis.*
Size 20in.
Habitat Grassland, woods, fields.
Distribution N America.
Food Insects and spiders.
Breeding Egg-laying and live-bearing in some areas.

VINE SNAKE

This snake has an elongated head and pointed snout. The color can be gray or brown, paler nearer the head. There is a dark line through the eye and a dark area on top of the head.

Scientific name *Oxybelis aeneus.*
Size 5ft.
Habitat Forest, scrub, trees.
Distribution S Arizona, S America, Mexico.
Food Lizards, amphibians.
Breeding Egg-laying, 3–5 eggs.

BULL SNAKE

A powerful snake with very keeled scales. The snout is pointed. There is a dark line running through each eye. The color is yellowish-brown with blotches which are either brown or rust-colored. If disturbed, this snake will hiss and may bite.

Scientific name *Pittuophis melanoleucus sayi.*
Size 8¹/₄ft.
Habitat Deserts, prairies, farmland.
Distribution N America to Mexico.
Food Small mammals, birds.
Breeding Egg-laying, up to 24 eggs.

8¹/₄ft

COMMON GARTER SNAKE

This species occurs farther north than any other snake in the New World. In the northernmost parts of its territory, it often congregates in huge numbers when hibernating.

Scientific name *Thamnophis sirtalis.*
Size 51in.
Habitat Farmland, prairies, near water.
Distribution N America.
Food Fish, ampihibians, earthworms.
Breeding Live-bearing, 7–85 young.

51in

TERRESTRIAL GARTER SNAKE

A large stocky snake, with keeled
scales. The markings can vary, but
there is often a stripe along the back
and on the flanks. Between the stripes,
the area can either be spotted and
pale, or dark with white blotches.

Scientific name *Thamnophis elegans.*
Size 39in.
Habitat Grasslands, wooded areas,
fields.
Distribution W USA.
Food Rodents, amphibians.
Breeding Live-bearing, 4–15 young.

WESTERN RIBBON SNAKE

A very slim snake with an orange stripe
down the middle of the back. There is a
cream or pale yellow stripe on each
flank. The color of the area between the
stripes is usually brown or olive. The
area around the mouth has light colored
scales.

Scientific name *Thamnophis proximus.*
Size 47in.
Habitat Woodlands, marshes, lake-
sides, tropical forests.
Distribution Gulf coast USA, Mexico,
Mississippi valley, C America.
Food Fish, frogs, insects, earthworms.
Breeding Live-bearing, 4–27 young.

DEATH ADDER

A bite from this snake can prove lethal to humans. This snake resembles a viper with a broad, triangular head, a short tail and lightly keeled scales. The color varies from gray, to red or brown, There are some crossbands over the body.

Scientific name *Acanthophis antarcticus.*
Size 20in.
Habitat Dry, rocky places.
Distribution Australia.
Food Small mammals, birds, reptiles.
Breeding Live-bearing, up to 20 young.

20in

BANDED KRAIT

A slim snake with a triangular cross-section to its body. Its head is narrow and the scales are smooth. The banded pattern alternates between black and white or cream, in bands of almost equal width. The pattern runs from the neck to the tail.

Scientific name *Bungarus fasciatus.*
Size 6^1/2ft.
Habitat Forests, fields.
Distribution SE Asia.
Food Other snakes.
Breeding Egg-laying.

6^1/2ft

BLACK MAMBA

A powerful snake with smooth scales and a narrow head. The color is dark gray, olive or brown – not black as the name would suggest. The head may have dark blotches and the mouth is black inside.

Scientific name *Dendroaspis polylepis.*
Size 8¹/₄ft.
Habitat Scrub, grassland.
Distribution Africa, southern half.
Food Small mammals, birds.
Breeding Egg-laying, 12–14 eggs.

TEXAS CORAL SNAKE

This snake is slim with smooth, shiny scales. The snout is black and there is a wide yellow band across the head. The rest of the body has red and black bands, separated by yellow bands.

Scientific name *Micrurus fulvius.*
Size 30in.
Habitat Sandy soil areas. Under logs.
Distribution SE USA, Mexico.
Food Snakes, lizards, small mammals.
Breeding Egg-laying, 3–5 eggs.

RINKALS or SPITTING COBRA

This snake can be marked with black bands on a gray, yellow or orange background. It can also be plain black or brown with specks of a paler color. When frightened, it rears up and spreads it hood out.

Scientific name *Hemachatus hemachatus.*
Size 39in.
Habitat Grassland.
Distribution S Africa.
Food Small mammals, birds, frogs, toads, reptiles.
Breeding Live-bearing, up to 63 young.

39in

INDIAN OR SPECTACLED COBRA

This snake has smooth scales and varies in color. They are usually black or dark brown, with lighter marks on the throat. When alarmed, it spreads out its hood very wide and can display a white mark, shaped like a 'spectacle', on the back.

Scientific name *Naja naja.*
Size 6¹/2ft.
Habitat Outskirts of villages and towns, farmland, forests.
Distribution India, Pakistan, Sri Lanka.
Food Small mammals, reptiles.
Breeding Egg-laying.

6¹/2ft

TIGER SNAKE

A snake with smooth scales. The color can be gray, olive or even reddish and there can be lighter crossbands. When alarmed, it can flatten out its neck, though they are normally a placid snake.

Scientific name *Notechis scutatus*.
Size 47in.
Habitat Forests, grassland.
Distribution SE Australia.
Food Frogs and small mammals.
Breeding Live-bearing, up to 100 young.

TAIPAN

A long snake with either smooth or keeled scales. The color can be either light or dark brown, which pales on the underside and flanks. The head is often a lighter color and can be cream.

Scientific name *Oxyuranus scutellatus*.
Size 6¹/₂ft.
Habitat Woodland, grassland, forests.
Distribution Australia, New Guinea.
Food Small mammals.
Breeding Egg-laying, 2–20 eggs.

FIERCE SNAKE

One of the most dangerous and venomous snakes in the world, though a rare species. A graceful snake with smooth scales, and large eyes. It is colored brown or olive and can have dark marks on the head. Similar to the Taipan but more deadly.

Scientific name *Oxyuranus microlepidotus.*
Size 6¹/₂ft.
Habitat Grassland, outback.
Distribution Central Australia.
Food Small mammals.
Breeding Egg Laying, 12–20 eggs.

6¹/₂ft

WESTERN BROWN SNAKE

A whip-like snake with a narrow head. The color varies considerably between light brown to black, and from solid colors to banded or crossbars. Combinations of these markings are also possible.

Scientific name *Pseudonaja nuchalis.*
Size 5ft.
Habitat Forests, grasslands, deserts.
Distribution Australia.
Food Small mammals, reptiles.
Breeding Egg-laying.

5in

BANDY BANDY

This is a burrowing venomous snake only found on the surface at night. The scales are smooth on this slim snake. The color is mainly black with white rings around the body and tail and across the head.

Scientific name *Vermicella annulata*.
Size 24in.
Habitat Wooded grasslands and scrub.
Distribution Australia.
Food Other snakes.
Breeding Egg-laying.

24in

PELAGIC SEA SNAKE

A very distinctive sea snake, which has hexagonal, non-overlapping scales. The head is elongated and the tail appears flattened. The color is a bright yellow with a dark line running along the back. They can be found in huge shoals in warm seas.

Scientific name *Pelamis platurus*.
Size 28in.
Habitat Marine.
Distribution African coast, S America, C America.
Food Fish.
Breeding Live-bearing.

28in

PUFF ADDER

A stocky snake with a wide, triangular head. The scales are very keeled and it has a short tail. The color can be brown or yellowish, with black chevron-shaped markings down the back. There is a white edge to each chevron. Markings can be indistinct.

Scientific name *Bitis arietans.*
Size 39in.
Habitat Most areas, except deserts.
Distribution Africa.
Food Small mammals, birds.
Breeding Live-bearing, 20–40 young.

39in

GABOON VIPER

A very large and stockily built snake. The head is broad, flat and triangular with small eyes. The patterning is geometric, made up of rectangles, triangles and diamonds. These act as camouflage on the forest floor. The colors can be buff, purple, pink and varieties of brown. Dangerous and venomous.

Scientific name *Bitis gabonica.*
Size 47in.
Habitat Forests.
Distribution Africa.
Food Medium mammals, birds.
Breeding Live-bearing, up to 60 young.

47in

RHINOCEROS VIPER

A stocky snake with heavily keeled scales. There are also horn-like scales on the snout. The coloring is made up of bluish-green, bow-tie marks on a purplish background. The sides are paler with marks edged in yellow.

Scientific name *Bitis nasicornis.*
Size 39in.
Habitat Forests, riverbanks.
Distribution W Africa.
Food Small mammals, birds.
Breeding Live-bearing.

NOSE-HORNED VIPER

A large viper with a fleshy horn on the snout. The scales are keeled and it is silvery-gray, brown or orange in color. There are darker zigzag markings which can appear to be separate blotches.

Scientific name *Vipera ammodytes.*
Size 39in.
Habitat Drystone walls, meadows, rocky areas.
Distribution Turkey, SE Europe.
Food Small mammals, birds.
Breeding Live-bearing, up to 10 young.

ADDER

A sturdy viper with some large scales on its head. There are keeled scales on the body. Males are gray with dark gray or black zigzag running down the back. Females are brown or reddish with a dark zigzag. Some species are pure black.

Scientific name *Vipera berus.*
Size 28in.
Habitat Bogs, woods, fields, heaths.
Distribution Europe, Asia.
Food Lizards, small rodents.
Breeding Live-bearing, up to 10 young.

28in

RUSSELL'S VIPER

A stocky snake which is pale gray-brown. There are dark brown ovals along the back which are edged in white. More ovals can be seen on the sides in an alternating pattern to those on the back.

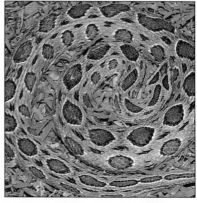

Scientific name *Vipera russelli.*
Size 39in.
Habitat Grasslands, plantations.
Distribution Pakistan, Burma, India, Sri Lanka.
Food Small Mammals.
Breeding Live-bearing, up to 65 young.

39in

LATASTE'S VIPER

A stoutly built viper with keeled scales. There is a fleshy horn on the snout. The color is gray or pale brown with a zigzag line running down the back. Down the sides, there are dark blotches.

Scientific name *Vipera latasti*.
Size 24in.
Habitat Hillsides which are stony, or sandy coastal places.
Distribution Spain, Portugal, Africa.
Food Small mammals, birds, lizards.
Breeding Live-bearing.

CANTIL

A viper with a long tail. The head is triangular with a white line running from the nose to the jaw. Another white line crosses the eyes. The body may be black or dark brown and there are wide bands of paler brown edged in white.

Scientific name *Agkistrodon bilineatus*.
Size 39in.
Habitat Scrub and forests.
Distribution Mexico.
Food Rodents.
Breeding Live-bearing, up to 10 young.

COPPERHEAD

This snake has keeled scales and a triangular head. The patterns are formed from bands of buff, pink or tan, alternating with bands of red, or brown. The tail may be tipped yellow in young snakes.

Scientific name *Agkistrodon contortrix.*
Size 30in.
Habitat Rocky hillsides, swamps.
Distribution SE USA (not Florida), Mexico.
Food Rodents, small birds, frogs.
Breeding Live-bearing, up to 8 young.

COTTONMOUTH

A large snake with keeled scales. There are crossbands within the brown, gray or black coloration. There can also be e thin white line from the snout to above the eye.

Scientific name *Agkistrodon piscivorus.*
Size 49in.
Habitat Rivers, ditches, swamps, lakes.
Distribution SE USA.
Food Fish, frogs, salamanders, small mammals, birds.
Breeding Live-bearing, 3–12 young.

PIT VIPERS

EYELASH VIPER

This is a tree dwelling snake which gets its name from a cluster of scales over each eye. A slim snake with very keeled scales. The color varies between yellow and green with brown marks resembling lichen.

Scientific name *Bothriopsis schlegelii*.
Size 24in.
Habitat Tropical rain forests.
Distribution S America.
Food Small birds, lizards, mammals.
Breeding Live-bearing.

STRIPED PALM VIPER

This pit viper has keeled scales and a wonderful color scheme. The head and neck are bluish-green with white spots or crossbars on the back. The young snakes are brown with black and white marks, before they alter to adult coloration.

Scientific name *Bothriechis lateralis*.
Size 28in.
Habitat Tropical forests.
Distribution Costa Rica, Panama.
Food Lizards, frogs, small mammals.
Breeding Live-bearing.

EASTERN DIAMONDBACK RATTLESNAKE

A large rattlesnake with a broad, rounded head. The coloring can be brown or olive with large, outlined diamonds down the back. The face has two colored streaks.

Scientific name *Crotalus adamanteus.*
Size 67in.
Habitat Pinewoods and palm scrub.
Distribution Florida.
Food Small mammals.
Breeding Live-bearing.

WESTERN DIAMONDBACK RATTLESNAKE

This large rattlesnake has a rounded snout. The diamonds on their backs are edged in a lighter color. The background color may be gray, bluish, pink or black. On the face, there are two light streaks, with a darker area in between.

Scientific name *Crotalus atrox.*
Size 67in.
Habitat Dry desert, grassland.
Distribution SW USA, N Mexico.
Food Rabbits, squirrels, rodents, birds.
Breeding Live-bearing, up to 40 young.

SOUTH AMERICAN RATTLESNAKE

This snake has a variety of species, colors and markings. The colors range from light gray, brown, yellow and tan, to greenish-gray olive and black. Several have diamond pattering on their backs, edged in yellow or white.

Scientific name *Crotalus durissus*.
Size 5ft.
Habitat Dry forests, grassland.
Distribution Mexico to Argentina.
Food Mammals, birds.
Breeding Live-bearing.

BLACK TAILED RATTLESNAKE

This snake has a varying pattern. It can be greenish, yellow, tan, orange or brown with diamonds along the back. The tail is black and there may be a black mark over the face.

Scientific name *Crotalus molossus*.
Size 39in.
Habitat Semi-desert, scrub, woods.
Distribution S USA, Central Mexico.
Food Small mammals, birds.
Breeding Live-bearing, 3–6 young.

P I T V I P E R S

RED DIAMONDBACK RATTLESNAKE

A slender rattlesnake with large, white edged, diamonds on its back. The colors can be brick-red, reddish-brown or orange. The tail has black and white rings before the rattle.

Scientific name *Crotalus ruber*.
Size 39in.
Habitat Deserts.
Distribution California, Mexico.
Food Small mammals, birds.
Breeding Live-bearing, 3–20 young.

MOJAVE RATTLESNAKE

A medium-sized rattlesnake often mistaken for other species. There are oval or diamond marks on the back. A light-colored stripe runs from the eye to the mouth.

Scientific name *Crotalus scutulatus*.
Size 39in.
Habitat Deserts, dry scrub, rocky places.
Distribution SW USA, central Mexico.
Food Small mammals.
Breeding Live-bearing, 2–11 young.

WESTERN RATTLESNAKE

There are several varieties of this snake. They all have a row of dark blotches on the back, which can be olive, brown or black. The background can be gray, cream, light green or buff.

Scientific name *Crotalus viridis.*
Size 5ft.
Habitat Deserts, forests, prairies.
Distribution W USA, N Mexico.
Food Small mammals, birds, reptiles.
Breeding Live-bearing, up to 25 young.

TIMBER RATTLESNAKE

Found in the Appalachians, this snake is one of the most common North American rattlesnakes. They may overwinter in large numbers in northern areas with other rat snakes. Colors vary between yellow or tan background with dark crossbars and a dusky black with little patterning.

Scientific name *Crotalus horridus.*
Size 47in.
Habitat Rocky slopes, wooded valleys.
Distribution Canada, USA.
Food Rodents, chipmunks.
Breeding Live-bearing.

WHITE-LIPPED PIT VIPER

A tree-living viper with a pale green color and orange eyes with vertical pupils. Yellowish-green underneath. There is a white line, along each side, in the male, which is absent in the female.

Scientific name *Trimeresurus albolabris*.
Size 28in.
Habitat Tropical forests.
Distribution NE India, SE China.
Food Lizards, frogs, rodents.
Breeding Live-bearing.

28in

WAGLER'S PIT VIPER

A distinctively colored, tree dwelling, pit viper. Adults are black with green spots, and green scales, edged in black on the sides. The young are green with red and white spots. The head is spade-shaped and black with yellowish-green streaks.

Scientific name *Tropidolaemus wagleri*.
Size 39in.
Habitat Tropical forests.
Distribution Thailand, Indonesia, Malaysia, Philippines.
Food Lizards, frogs, small mammals.
Breeding Live-bearing.

39in

Index   Index of common names

INDEX

Index Index of scientific names